The Simplicity of Autism

Good News and Practical Truth

Tony Rice

United States Copyright registered.

TABLE OF CONTENTS

Preface 6

Chapter 1
Autism Is... Essential 12

Chapter 2
My Story *Take 3 21

Chapter 3
TJ's Story 46

Chapter 4
Autism Diagnosis, A Short History 63

Chapter 5
Autism in Basic Terms 70

Chapter 6
One 73

Chapter 7
Experts are - Human 80

Chapter 8
You can See It 84

Chapter 9
Common Sound Experiences 90

Chapter 10
Cure V/S Acceptance 94

Chapter 11
Knock-Knock, Who IS in There?........................... 99

Chapter 12
Be Right There 106

Chapter 13
Agitated or Busy? 110

Chapter 14
Another Take 114

Chapter 15
Language.. 116

Chapter 16
Need to be Right 128

Chapter 17
Dig for the Diamond 132

Chapter 18
"I am So Sorry?" 135

Chapter 19
The Numbers... 138

Chapter 20
The Workplace 141

Chapter 21
Thank You 145

DEDICATION

I dedicate this book to my son, TJ and to my daughter, Courtney.

You are champions through adversity. I am so proud of you both, and I adore you.

PREFACE

Have you ever had that dream, the one where you are next to somebody that you care about? You need to say something important, but you are unable to make a sound. You are not mad or angry in this dream, you love this person. You are so close to them, yet you feel invisible.

This dream scenario helps to explain why I am compelled to write this book. As one who is both a father of an Autistic dude, and as one who is also on the Spectrum, I am sharing with you a series of world views and perspective that come from behind the eyes of Autism. Views and perspective that are safe. Views and perspective that are infused with love, hope and optimism. This book is a guilt free zone!

The focus of my book is about the humanity of Autism. This book offers unapologetic and optimistic insight into a mysterious life experience that, in truth, is not mysterious at all.

This book is not about treating, counseling, intervening, curing, or changing any person who is on the Autism Spectrum. There are many, many good people who dedicate their lives to doing much of what I have described above, but that is not my mission.

This book is a good news story about Autism.

Wouldn't it be great if you could encounter an Autistic individual in a **casual setting**, possessing full confidence that you know what you are looking at? Not cautiously timid, not a little bit taken aback, I mean completely comfortable and assured in your ability to connect with that individual on a personal level.

Wouldn't it be great if you, as an **employer** could be completely confident as you interact with, manage, and collaborate with any Autistic individual who might share your work environment.

And **parents**, when you receive a new Autism diagnosis for your child, a diagnosis that you never contemplated, and that you never would have anticipated, wouldn't it be great to possess immediate confidence, clarity and conviction as to how you will advocate with, walk with, support and love your child through this unplanned life journey?

There is nothing wrong with diving headlong into the researching of detached, generic data points about this thing called Autism. Research is a good thing. It is just not the most important thing. Not by a long shot.

When my son was diagnosed, I questioned if I really knew who he was. Suddenly, it seemed like I needed an expert to tell me who he was. I felt like I did not have a confident grasp on anything at that point.

I was, however, wrong. I had it backwards. I knew full well who my son was and who he is, but with the introduction of an Autism Spectrum Diagnosis, I initially questioned everything.

Today, when I read new information, attend conferences or view informative videos about Autism, I understand that this sort of information can help me better understand elements of *nuance* about my son.

No expert, no study or educational video can tell me **who** my son is. That is an inside job, and my son is counting on me to make that job my highest priority and my first priority.

When I do my job well, then we can evaluate any new information that might specifically benefit our life journey. Knowing, understanding, accepting and embracing my son as my first priority assures that we will retain new information that is helpful, and also that we will enthusiastically leave behind information that is unhelpful.

This is the first book that you should read if you are encountering Autistic individuals at any level of relationship in your daily life.

This book is the first book that any employer should read before you hire, manage and/or work with any individual on the Autism Spectrum.

And parents, yes, when you get that initial Autism Diagnosis for your child, please read this book before you do anything else.

Over the past three and one-half years, I have conducted more than 6,000 focus groups on the topics that are covered within this book. In that process I have been able to speak to hundreds of parents of Autistic individuals along with dozens of psychologists, neurologists, behavior analysts, teachers, and other trained specialists.

I have spoken to thousands of individuals who know somebody, a friend, or a relative of an individual who is on the Autism Spectrum. I have also spoken to many individuals, who like my son, and me, are on the Autism Spectrum.

In the beginning, I was timid about my views relating to the Simplicity of Autism. I approached every conversation from the angle of, "What am I missing here?". The feedback, the hope and affirmation that have resulted from these conversations has given me assurance that this message is one that can and will change lives for the better.

Based on extensive research and based on decades of personal life experience, I have some game-changing information to share with you; information that will take the Autism conversation to a remarkably better place.

Chapter 1

Autism Is... Essential

Through my process of preparing for, and for writing this book, I have been able to engage in thousands of first-encounter conversations about the topics that are addressed within this book. Those conversations have been with people that represent many different walks of life.

I continue to have those conversations daily as I near the completion of this book. One such conversation that happened last week compelled me to make this chapter the first chapter in my book rather than the last chapter in my book.

I will get to introductions shortly, but before I do that, I ask that you try to imagine planet earth without the remarkable influences and contributions from individuals who are on the Autism Spectrum.

It is hard, probably impossible, to imagine life as we know it without those influences and contributions.

With that in mind, I have listed in this chapter a number of contributions to humanity that have come from individuals who are on the Autism Spectrum.

A note - be sure to read this chapter to the end. This book is first and foremost about the *humanity* of individuals on the Autism Spectrum. Gifts and accomplishments are important, but not most important.

Please read, contemplate and enjoy.

Autism is essential if:

Autism is essential if you love your smart phone. Just ask **Steve Jobs**.

Autism is essential if you value the humane treatment of animals as a priority within the beef processing industry, just ask **Temple Grandin**.

Autism is essential if you like actors that shock and scare you. Just ask **Anthony Hopkins**.

Autism is essential if you ever wonder, "Who ya gonna call?" Just ask **Dan Akroyd**.

Autism is essential if you have benefited from an intuitive computer operating system today. Just ask **Bill Gates.**

Autism is essential if you are moved by a famous painting titled, A Starry Night. Just ask **Vincent Van Gogh.**

Autism is essential if you love the creative energy and vibrant colors that are pop art. Just ask **Andy Warhol.**

Autism is essential if you are a lover of late 20th century New Wave music. Just ask **David Byrne,** lead song writer and singer for the band, Talking Heads.

Autism is essential if you were mesmerized by the creative brilliance that is the movie, Edward Scissorhands. Just ask producer **Tim Burton.**

Autism is essential if you like to get the bejeebies scared out of you. Just ask the producer of the movie, The Shining, **Stanley Kubrick.**

Autism is essential if you were entertained by the 1984 popular movie, Splash. Just ask the famous actress, **Darryl Hannah.**

Autism is essential if you are moved by the music of the 1960's breakthrough folk music icon and legend, **Bob Dylan**.

Autism is essential if your heart has been warmed by ET's touching plea to *phone home*, just ask **Steven Spielberg**.

Autism is essential if you relied on electricity today, just ask **Benjamin Franklin**.

Autism is essential if the theories of gravity, light and energy have had impact in your lives, just ask **Albert Einstein**.

Autism is essential if you have enjoyed recorded music or electric lighting today, just ask **Thomas Edison**.

Autism is essential if The Gettysburg Address has inspired you to live a life of purpose. Just ask **Abraham Lincoln**.

Autism is essential if you believe great leadership made possible the winning of the Revolutionary War, and the establishment of the first presidency of the United States of America, just ask **George Washington**.

Autism is essential if you have appreciated the amazing frescoes that are the glorious body of art contained within the Sistine Chapel, just ask **Michaelangelo**.

Autism is essential if your heart has ever soared with the magnificent symphony, The Requiem in D Minor, just ask **Wolfgang Amadeus Mozart**.

Autism is essential if you were encouraged in your childhood by the inspirational fable, The Ugly Duckling. Just ask **Hans Christian Anderson**.

Autism is essential if you are one who appreciates inspirational American poetry born of the mid to late 1800's, just ask **Emily Dickenson**.

Autism is essential if the alternating current that powers most homes, and every appliance within most homes makes your life better. Just ask **Nicholas Tesla**.

I will also make honorable mention of two additional Founding Fathers of America, **Thomas Jefferson** and **Alexander Hamilton**.

What an amazing array of individuals who have advanced quality of our lives in immeasurable ways. Surely, there are others that I am missing, but I know that you get the point here.

Alas, I acknowledge that the suggested questioning of many of these historical figures will be of a rhetorical nature only. For those who lived before a modern medical diagnosis for Autism was available, and for many who are no longer here, these assertions to the presence of Autism are taken from detailed biographical accounts.

Based on my research, and of the research of many others, the documented traits and idiosyncrasies associated with these individuals speaks profoundly to the evidence of Autism.

I am convinced, but you may not be. If that is the case, might I suggest that you and I meet up at the nearest nerd bar, research in hand, grab a stiff whole milk and rumble!

Joking aside, I am personally convinced with each example of the Autistic individuals that I have listed. And, it goes without saying, this is a very empowered list!

Plus, consider this. This listing is one that only addresses notable celebrities and historical figures. Contemplate for a moment the scores of other individuals on the Autism Spectrum who have created or influenced countless products and processes towards the advancement of humanity.

It boggles the mind in a very good way. Yes, Autism is essential.

One final note on this chapter. I am acknowledging that, of course, there are many on the Autism Spectrum that have sensory impacts to a degree that they will more than likely not be inventors or innovators towards the advancement of modern society. Many on the Spectrum are non-verbal, many will need daily supports throughout life.

With that in mind, I will share with you my personal ranking of Autistic individuals as it relates to making planet earth an infinitely better place.

1) My most influential group of individuals on the Autism Spectrum are those most impacted by their Autism Diagnosis. These are the people who remind us of what really matters in this life, and of what really does not matter in this life. In my view, this is not even a close call. These Autistic individuals provide the most important and the most life affirming messages towards the elevation of humanity.
2) The countless, unnamed or unknown individuals who are on the Autism Spectrum who are responsible for so many of the daily life quality resources that seamlessly and quietly elevate our life experience.
3) The famous and historical individuals that I have listed within this chapter. These are people who are fewer in number, but they have provided major impacts to life experience and to life quality that far exceed their numbers.

There you go. Those who might be viewed as the least among us are truly the greatest among us.

As it should be.

As it is.

Introductions

Chapter 2

My Story - "Take 3"

As a parent of a 28-year-old dude on the Autism Spectrum, and as a 58-year-old guy who was also diagnosed on the Spectrum nine years ago, my life is one that has had its moments.

This is my third take at telling my story as a part of this book. I had planned to skip my story completely. The message of this book is optimistic, encouraging and hopeful.

As I read other books that share a similar purpose, to inform and to inspire, I realized that on some level, I need to share with you who I am and why I am the one who is writing this book.

I want you to know that I am really ok if you choose to skip reading this chapter of this book. I feel obligated to share with you who the writer is so that you can know more detail about the writer, but other than helping to explain where my passion and drive for change comes from, my story is not the focus of this book.

In my first attempt to tell my story, I went into a lot of detail. By the time I was finished, my story amounted to 41 pages. It was a book all in and of itself.

So, I scrapped it, and I re-wrote my story. I tried to streamline the story. I failed! Final count, 51 pages on my second try.

With all of that, the following is my best attempt at a condensed version of my story for now.

Here goes:

My early life story includes elements and events that occurred in the depths of suicidal depression, leading to alcoholism, that you may be surprised to read about in a book like this

Sometimes, I slow down and I take myself back to that earlier life. This was a life that was pre-Autism diagnosis. This was a life that was distorted and confusing for me. I felt different, but I had no idea why. I was vulnerable and I was in many ways, rudderless.

I have always had an intense emotional awareness. This means that the life affirming moment that happens in pretty much any movie, reality music show, or Sponge Bob episode for that matter, can get me misty eyed, or worse, at the drop of a hat.

I also seem to have this super-power of reading people with dishonest or manipulative motives instantly. I pegged my Dad at the age of 4, more on that later.

If your talk does not match your motives, I don't just notice it, I feel it, intensely. I believe that this is for me, simply an Autism trait. It is this trait that compelled me to write this book.

Looking back, I can see that my Autism traits were mostly masked earlier in my life. They began to emerge in my late teens and early twenties. I had no idea what was happening. Being a chemically depressive person by nature, I blamed myself, severely, for everything in my life that seemed to be going wrong.

Words like hopeless and useless really did not apply to me at that point because those words were words that applied to *human beings*. My perception at that point about myself was that I was sub-human and/or non-human.

I think that this is the best that I can do in terms of describing the lost and spiraling nature of my life at that time.

I never would have believed, at that time, that I could have crossed over from that dark side of life, to this side of life. My journey towards wholeness and healing has been anything but quick. My life today is unrecognizable when compared to that earlier life. And of course, my lifelong journey towards understanding, healing and wholeness continues.

Today, I am grateful for my journey, all of it. I have, and I continue to take it all to God, to the best of my ability. I know that God will take everything that I bring to Him, and He will use it for good.

I heard a speaker recently who noted that our greatest wisdom does not materialize at the summit, that wisdom only comes through the valleys that we travel and the hills that we climb.

Those dark experiences of my life have become my greatest gifts to encourage and to serve others today.

I just wanted to offer some sort of a heads-up to prepare you for some darker elements in my story.

I was the third boy born to parents that were both under twenty years old at the time of my birth.

I was diagnosed with a bone disease called Osteochondroma at the age of four. The disease causes extra bones to grow, often in joint areas like knees and wrists. It was also believed that I had a high likelihood of getting bone cancer.

Ultimately, by the age of 13, I had 9 corrective surgeries. No bone cancer.

Our parents divorced when I was in the 2nd grade.

I had total clarity, at the age of 4, that my father was a sociopath. Sociopath is actually a nickname for *anti-social personality disorder*. I did not have clarity about that sort of vocabulary at the time, but I was on point with the sentiment.

At the time that my parents divorced, we were offered the choice of who we would live with. I jumped in quickly and said I wanted to live with Mom. My brothers wanted to return, from Florida to Alabama, and live with Dad. I was told that the kids should not be separated, so I needed to live with Dad too.

My parents re-married about one year later. For the year that they were divorced, we boys lived through a lot of darkness.

Our home was almost never an emotionally safe place. We just never knew what Dad was going to do. When my surgeries would happen, our family would seem to briefly become normal and safe. As the years went by, I began to hope that my periodic check-ups would require surgeries. The reward of emotional safety at home was worth it.

Our little brother, Chris was born when I was 11 years old. During the time of Mom's pregnancy, that was a mostly safe and normal time too. I didn't trust my father, but I did appreciate the respite from emotional chaos that happened during those months.

Chris, our younger brother brought a lot of life, light and laughter to the family. Financially, things were always tight.

I joined the marching band in junior high school, and I learned how to play the trumpet pretty quickly. I was 1st chair soloist in the marching band.

One afternoon, shortly after I had a knee surgery, I was walking really slowly and in pain, truthfully, a lot of pain, across the back of the band room. I felt invisible to the world at that moment, so I didn't expect that anybody would notice me.

My band director, Eugene Cook, was one of the most humble and most esteemed human beings that I have ever known. He was African American, and we were in the deep south. *Two years prior, Alabama State Troopers armed with machine guns had lined the halls of our junior high school. This was at the height of the segregation movement. That racism stuff never resonated with me, or with my family, and I am grateful for that.*

I glanced over at Mr. Cook from the back of the band room, and I saw that he was watching me. Closely. A tear was running down his cheek. That powerful expression of love, coming from a man that I respected and admired so greatly, really impacted me. To this day, I tear up every time I think about it. I needed that kind of love in my life, and somehow, he knew it.

I came to a Christian faith in junior high school I attended a Bible Study each morning in the school lunchroom. Sometimes, I even led that Bible Study.

My understanding of theology was pretty thin, but I was all in with my faith in Christ.

During my 3 years of middle school, my life had wholeness and purpose. I began to wander away from my Christian faith when I moved on to high school.

When I was entering the 11th grade of high school, my dad accepted a job with Boeing in Seattle, Washington. My two older brothers both had athletic scholarships at a local, well regarded private school. They stayed in our hometown and lived with our grandmother while Chris, my little brother, and I moved with Mom and Dad to Seattle.

In Seattle, I started to experience anxiety, and it really perplexed me. I had one date while I was there, with a girl who I was not really interested in. For the whole date, I was totally overwhelmed with anxiety and I had no idea why.

My father was transferred to Wichita, KS at the end of that year. I moved back home to live with my grandmother, and I attended my original high school for my senior year and graduation.

I went heavy into drugs and alcohol during that summer before my senior year of high school. I was also in some dangerous situations that summer. One that narrowly avoided gun fire, and it was me who was reaching for the gun. Our car was surrounded by a large group, and we were going to be dragged out of the car. A park ranger drove up in the dark of night, seconds before I reached for it, and we were able to get out of that situation.

During my senior year of high school, I started having enormous and devastating anxiety attacks daily. I had a sweet, Christian girlfriend who didn't know how to help me. I started living a double life, evenings spent with her and her family, and late nights with my drinking and drugging people.

I didn't know what was happening, but it was destroying me. My girlfriend broke up with me at the end of that school year and I started down a path of suicidal depression.

I moved to Wichita, Kansas, to live with my oldest brother and my mother when I was 20 years old.

Anxiety and depression consumed my life. I drank and smoked pot most evenings, alone. I had three encounters with prostitutes, while drunk, during that time. I also narrowly escaped getting stabbed at a roughneck bar.

After a short trip with my oldest brother, Olen, back to our hometown in Alabama, the floor completely fell out from under me. On that trip back to familiar surroundings, I recognized how low I had fallen in life in comparison to my earlier years in my hometown.

That realization was my last straw. I was finished. The following day, after we returned to Wichita, my only question was how to take my life. I planned on getting drunk and then swerving my VW bug in front of a dump truck. It seemed like that would be quick and nobody else would get hurt.

I went for a walk around our block that morning, in full despair and tears, and then another miracle happened.

My brother was a meter reader for the electric company, along with being a full-time student. He was assigned a new route each morning, and that route could have been located anywhere within a 50-mile radius of Wichita.

On that morning, his route was located in our neighborhood, on my block. He rounded the corner and before I saw him, he saw me. He saw everything that I had been hiding. He saw that I needed help, and he made arrangements for me to meet with a dept. of mental health intake counselor right away.

I met with that intake counselor and I was actually surprised when he said that he was referring me to a therapist for long term care. Denial is a deceptive element of depression. Even with all that had happened and all that was happening, it shocked me that I was in need of mental health care.

My therapist was a woman. She was attractive and kind. In hindsight, she was also really good.

For months, I would go, and talk. I didn't see where any of it was going, at that point, I was just attending sessions because I didn't want to hurt my family.

About 6 months into the therapy, I got really drunk on a Saturday night, and I had my last encounter with a prostitute. Before I started therapy, there had been two encounters, but I was shocked that it happened again.

I was sure that my therapist would tell me to leave her office when I told her what had happened. When we met, I told her. I braced for her disgusted reaction, but that didn't happen. Not only did she not judge me, she responded to me with empathy.

I saw my first ray of hope in that moment. For 6 months, our sessions had felt directionless.

She had been patiently waiting for me to discover, on my own terms, however long that would take, that I could trust her.

I made big progress in my recovery from depression over the next 6 months. Interestingly, at that time, medications were not really a thing. If I were in that same situation today, medication would have been a key part of the process, no doubt.

I am sure that my recovery was made more difficult without medication, but somehow, today I feel like that enhanced struggle has benefitted me. At the age of 57, I took my first anti-depressant. The medication is really helpful for me. I had no idea, prior to taking medication, that I was burning up so much of my energy each day, simply doing battle with the chemical imbalance related to depression within my brain. Medication is good science, and I highly recommend it to any who might benefit.

My life circumstances required that I relocate to Huntsville Alabama after an additional six months of therapy while in Wichita.

When I arrived in Huntsville, I made arrangements to see a new therapist. She was a rough and tumble, gravelly voice, cigarette puffing lady.

She looked at me and said, "You look great, what da ya wanna do in your life?".

At that time, my depression was a lot better, but I still had enormous anxiety about being around other people, especially in any sort of confined room.

I told her, I want to try and take a course at the local junior college. When I said it, I couldn't believe I was saying it. At that time, it was really an unthinkable thing for me to do.

The therapist replied, "Well then, go do it!". That was my first and last session with her.

I did apply for a class at the junior college and I attended the first 3 classes. That was all that I could do, but for me, it was a huge victory.

I spent the next 3 years in Huntsville, mostly just getting used to being alive and present, and learning to be among people again.

I had very little money during that time, but I would save up so that I could get drunk every other week. Drinking as a form of self-medication became central to my life as years went by.

I relocated to Milwaukee, Wisconsin. My brother had taken a sales job in Wisconsin and he invited me to live with him and his wife Julie while I attended college.

I bartended for income, and I attended the University of Wisconsin-Milwaukee. Over 2 years, I earned about 1 years-worth of college credits. I dabbled in school, and I excelled in drinking.

I bailed from college after 2 years, and I followed my brother into the arena of selling toys and sporting goods to mass merchant retailers.

I got married at the age of 28, and we had our first child when I was 29 years old.

My job took us to St. Charles, Missouri when TJ, our boy was 3 months old. We began to notice at around the age of 2, that TJ's developmental milestones were happening differently than for other kids.

TJ was placed in an early childhood program at the age of 3. We also learned that, genetically, I had transferred my bone disease to him. TJ had his first surgery at the age of 3. His Osteochondroma case has involved a lot more complications than I experienced. As of this writing he has had 26 surgeries.

Courtney, our daughter was born 21 months after TJ. During the pregnancy for her, we were told after an ultra-sound check up, that she appeared to have a chromosome issue. Mary, my ex-wife, was in tears as we drove home from the doctor's appointment. I don't know where this came from within me, but I told her, "God doesn't create tragedies. Whatever is in store for us, we can be sure that it will be very, very good." I was not a religious guy at that time.

At our next prenatal visit, we received good news. Our baby was perfectly healthy, they were wrong about the chromosome anomaly.

Statistically, Courtney was supposed to have no chance of getting Osteochondroma. She defied the odds. As of this writing, Courtney has had 9 surgeries as well.

When the kids were young, I was traveling a lot for work. Mary, my ex-wife needed for me to be at home. I resigned from my traveling sales position and I opened an independent shipping, mailing and printing center, similar to a Fed-Ex Kinkos business.

That business struggled in the beginning, but then it did quite well.

Mary and I had been in marriage counseling for 5 years, and at that point. I concluded at that time, that we should divorce.

The divorce was really hard on TJ and Courtney. I don't believe the scars of divorce can ever fully heal. I can only love my kids relentlessly, to respect and support their process, and to walk with them through all of it. That is what I do. Although I don't question the divorce, I live with guilt about it every day. I guess that never goes away.

I sold the business because I could not run it and be there for my kids to the degree that our family circumstances required.

After I sold the business, I had a pocket full of money for a while. I found myself drinking 12 to 18 beers nightly. Most of that drinking occurred when the kids were at their mom's house, or after I put the kids to bed.

On September 6th, 2002, my little brother, Chris, died in a car crash. He was 29 years old. He was an RCA recording artist, and an amazing talent.

I believe that he also dealt with some of the demons that I have known.

Chris had been in recovery from alcohol and substance abuse for a full year before getting signed, with his band, by RCA. He had been in the gym every day, and he was in really great shape.

After getting signed, he started drinking a little. In no time, he was back into the throes of addiction.

I think there may be some debate in my family whether Chris's fatal crash was an accident or intentional. As a survivor of suicidal depression, I believe that he snapped in the moment. He aimed his car for the only telephone pole within ½ mile of the accident scene.

Right before he hit the telephone pole, like many who survive suicide attempts have shared, he realized that he didn't really want to die. He locked up the brakes and he turned the wheel hard to the right. It was too late. He hit the telephone pole, snapped it in two, and he was ejected through the front windshield.

I had spoken to him earlier that day. He sounded like he was in rough shape from a late hard night of drinking. Later that day, after we spoke, he and his band recorded a song titled, "Beyond the Sun". The lyrics of that song read to me as his suicide letter.

Chris's band was called 3AE. You can find "Beyond the Sun" and other 3AE songs on YouTube. The song is powerful. *(Their producer, Tony Battaglia, is also the producer for the band Shinedown. As evidence of the hidden ugliness that is prominent within the music industry, Battaglia later recorded and released that song with Shinedown, with the claim that he and Brent Smith, lead singer for Shinedown, wrote that song. Pretty sick. Shinedown's (stolen) version is on YouTube too. Chris's version is so, so much better, for obvious reasons.)*

On January 11, 2004, I surrendered to the fact that I am an alcoholic. I entered recovery, and by God's grace, I have not needed to take a drink of alcohol, or any other mind altering substance, since that day.

For the next several years, I was spending a lot of time at TJ's school. Financially, this was really tough. In my previous traveling sales job, it was common to dine at some of the finest restaurants in the world.

As a single dad, spending way too much time at school, we learned how food pantries work and the electricity was not always turned on.

My recovery sponsor once told me that I needed to back off and let the professionals, the teachers and the counselors, do their job. I considered what he had suggested for 24 hours, and then I told him, "If the stress of advocating for my son is going to cause me to relapse into alcoholism and die, then I am just going to need to relapse and die. I can't abandon my son to people who are emotionally harming him because they do not understand what is happening with him".

I expected that my recovery sponsor would tell me to go and find another sponsor. Instead, he saw that I was being sincere and authentic. He understood that I was not using the chaos of Autism advocacy as a convenient escape from reality.

The issues with the local public-school system only got worse. Midway through the 6th grade, with some amazing help from my oldest brother and my mother, I was able to get TJ into one of the best therapeutic schools in the country, Logos School – Ladue, MO.

I missed even more work that first year at Logos School. TJ would be sent home, usually 2 or 3 days each week for behavior issues. He was really angry about what he had endured in the public school, and there was a process of acting out and learning from each behavior event. After that 1st year at Logos School, TJ was sent home only once over the next 5 years. *A kid had cornered TJ, and TJ bopped that kid in the nose.*

TJ attended a public school for his senior year, and he graduated high school in 2010.

TJ and I moved to Kansas City in 2011, I had a ground floor opportunity in a start-up company, and I was able to travel again at that point.

At 7 years into my recovery with alcoholism, I returned to my Christian faith. I prove every day that I am saved by Grace, and not by my exemplary Christian performance. My faith, and serving others, means everything to me today.

While I was in Kansas City, I entered into a relationship, and then was married to a beautiful person and a beautiful soul, Tracy. To be honest, I am still unpacking what happened there. I was not emotionally available to her in the way that she deserved, and my advocacy for TJ, and for my daughter Courtney, seemed to push anything else out of my life.

Tracy and I divorced two years later. She and I remain dear and loving friends, and that will always be the case.

TJ and I relocated to Plano, Texas in 2014. He was becoming unfulfilled and depressed while working in a grocery store in Kansas City. I had learned of a tech program for young adults on the Autism Spectrum, located within the Southern Methodist University – Plano, Texas Campus.

That program was helpful for TJ, but it was not the pathway to career and income that he was seeking.

TJ now works full time in a light manufacturing position. He has a job coach that is provided through a wonderful organization called My Possibilities-Launchability, also located in Plano, Texas.

I took a position as a sales manager for a Hong Kong based toy manufacturer shortly after arriving in Texas. That position required me to make 6 to 7 trips to Hong Kong and China each year.

I started driving for Uber, basically anytime that I was not traveling, shortly after we arrived here in Texas. It helped to cover the bills from the move and the programs. I didn't plan to, or expect to, but for some reason, I began to talk to nearly every rider about Autism, and about this idea of the Simplicity of Autism.

In 2017, I was listening to my Pastor, Jeff Jones. He was talking about the idea that many people become invested in a career through years of blood, sweat and tears.

Many times, we realize that a career is not aligned with our talents, abilities and/or passions, but we stay in that career anyway. We conclude that we just have too much invested to walk away.

He finished his thought by saying, "But here's the thing. You will *never* be great at that career".

He hit me square between the eyes with that last comment. I was experienced and proficient in the world of mass retail sales. I also knew that I was in the wrong place.

I resigned my Sales Manager position in December of 2018, and I became certified as a Special Needs Life Quality Coach. Once I became a coach, I realized that I should complete this book as my first step into coaching and into public speaking on the theme of *The Simplicity of Autism*.

For now, I continue to do focus groups and networking while driving Uber. My message continues to get clearer and stronger. This week alone, I have had dozens of incredible conversations. Daily, people thank me for offering helpful new awareness and insights about Autism.

I really am an unlikely vessel to deliver this message of hope and promise. That said, God has a long history of using rickety vessels like me as conduits for Him. This really is His doings, not mine. I am just grateful to have a good seat to watch His show.

My life story is messy. For many years, I tried to make sense of this world, and of my life, without the realization that I too am on the Autism Spectrum.

It has taken every bit of trouble, struggle and chaos in my life to bring me clarity as to what really matters, and to also understand what really does not matter.

The unexpected outcome of my twisted journey is this message that I hope can and will help so many.

Chapter 3

TJ's Story

I am intentionally not going into detail in this book about my co-parenting relationship with TJ's mother, Mary.

She and I have shared many agreements along the way regarding TJ's best life path, and we have had disagreements too.

The focus of this book is The Simplicity of Autism. With that, I don't think that it serves a purpose to reflect and or to debate those issues within this book.

TJ's mother, Mary, loves TJ dearly.

TJ was born on March 21st, 1992. He was meeting common developmental milestones up until age two. Right around that time, he became mostly non-verbal. We later learned that this was an early indicator of his regressive Autism diagnosis.

At first, I thought that he might have a hearing impairment because he seemed to be less responsive to verbal communication. I would stand by his bedroom door and whisper to check for his reaction. He would react to my whispers, so I knew his changes were not hearing related.

He was very focused and passionate about his Hot Wheels car collection. He would meticulously line 100's of cars up with perfect parallel spacing. He was also passionate about real cars, American Muscle Cars most notably. Cars were the one topic that he talked about often. Other than that, he had little to say between the ages of two and three.

At around the age of three, he was diagnosed with my bone condition, Multiple Hereditary Osteochondroma.

His first corrective bone surgery was scheduled when he was three years old. I felt personally responsible and I was full of guilt. This was happening to him because of me.

TJ and I spent the night in the hospital as he was scheduled for his surgery early the following morning.

That evening, we were playing in the pediatric playroom and we met a four-year old little guy that had just been diagnosed with an aggressive form of brain cancer. His aunt was with him and she explained to me what was happening with him. His diagnosis was terminal.

We played together with that little guy for quite a while. We laughed and we had some good fun. I was thinking, this little guy is not dead yet. Let's honor his dignity. He is very much alive, and I know that he wants to be treated that way.

That experience put my guilt and despair about TJ's, and Courtney's bone conditions in a different perspective. I never diminished or minimized the pain that he or his sister endured from their surgeries. I did, however, develop an attitude of gratitude about the fact that I get to take my kids home from the hospital after their surgeries. Not everybody is as fortunate.

We did not and we have not entertained pity. Pity has no place in my life, and it definitely has no place in my kid's lives. We have had life challenges, and by leaning on the strength of God, we have met those challenges.

TJ began to attend an early childhood development program beginning at the age of four. The focus was for him to develop in the area of language. We did not have an official Autism diagnosis at that point.

At that time, I would say to his teachers, "Learning about the subject of language is good, but he is *experiencing* this place differently, there is more to this than a language issue".

Entering into elementary school, we were really lost and directionless. We were introduced to this thing called an IEP(Individualized Educational Program). There was a team of people who told us they were going to help our son.

The IEP plan was focused on an idea of inclusion, but there really was no inclusion plan. The plan in actuality was, "When TJ acts "differently", he will be removed from the classroom, and placed in the cross-category room".

The cross-category room was a place where kids with significant mental retardation were kept. That room essentially entailed monitoring them and keeping them from escaping.

At one point during his first-grade year, an emergency meeting was called. We were told that TJ was having violent fantasies and that we needed to talk about it right away.

In that quickly arranged IEP meeting, there were six or eight long faces staring at us as we waited to start. I had no idea what we were about to hear. I felt a pit in my stomach.

The meeting started. They began to describe TJ's fascination with shotguns, and with shooting cars. At some point, somebody mentioned that TJ was talking about shooting a radiator.

I asked them, "Has anybody here seen the Disney movie, The Fox and the Hounds?" Nobody answered.

I explained the scene in that movie where the nice old lady threatens to shoot the cantankerous old man's radiator out if he tried to harm the fox.

At that point, everybody got it. It bothered me that they went to such a dark assumption about TJ, so quickly. But more than anything, I was relieved.

TJ ended up spending most of his first-grade year contained in that cross-category room. We were told to be prepared for the idea that institutionalization might be in his future. I told them that I really thought they were wrong.

We moved to another elementary school for the next four years. TJ was assigned a para-professional, but only after I threatened to remove him from that school system.

The new school was better, but it was far from good. Utilization of a cross-category room was removed from his IEP plan. The behavior director at that school, however, did utilize a locked/padded room several times during his second-grade year. The padded room was considered a "last alternative" if TJ would not comply and "calm down".

We put an end to the padded room after a few episodes. Although some progress was made at the new elementary school, TJ became increasingly frustrated. The behavior director, nearing his retirement, operated on the belief that TJ was responsive to his "loud and booming" voice.

By the end of his time at that elementary school, TJ was pretty much ready to kill that guy. When your sensory intensities are already enhanced fifty to one hundred times greater than average, loud noises are anything but calming and centering.

Full disclosure: TJ had a para-professional through middle of his sixth-grade school year, and it was not successful. TJ hated being treated differently than the other students. The presence of the para-professional became highly embarrassing to him.

We endured elementary school, and then we looked for a fresh start as we moved on to middle school for his 6th grade school year.

The middle school behavior director and IEP team offered the promise of a better and more effective approach.

This did not happen.

During the ½ year that TJ attended at his new middle school, I found myself at school most days of each week. I would arrive at my work, get a phone call from the behavior director, and be right back over at the school.

I could never tolerate the situation where I knew the school staff was getting frustrated at TJ because they were not understanding what was happening with him. I had to be there, and on many days, the only good option was to take him home.

The middle school experience soon began to look a lot like the elementary school experience.

Frequent special IEP team meetings were called. In these meetings, the theme was repetitive, "TJ would just not get with the plan". The *plan* was essentially for TJ act and appear to be like the other kids. That was not inclusion, that was pretending. That was also dehumanizing.

Our public education system in the early 2000's was just not prepared for Autistic students.

During one of those special IEP meetings, the staff was going on about how TJ would not get with the plan, and of the blue, I blurted out, "Why don't we just flip it?". They said, what are you talking about? I said, "Let's just flip it, let's just force every other kid in this school to pretend to live within TJ's sensory reality". My comment was not well received, and I said, "Exactly!".

The school district had hired a purported Autism expert away from The Judevine Center. The Judevine Center was, at the time, a nationally recognized pioneering Autism research organization based in the St. Louis area.

When our school district recruited him away from The Judevine Center, it is safe to say that Judevine did not lose one of its most valued assets.

This "expert" consistently placed the priorities of the school district ahead of TJ's needs. He lobbied to have TJ assigned to the "behavior building", a separate annex that was exclusively created for violent/emotionally disturbed students. TJ was plenty frustrated, but he had never been violent, not once.

With all of this going on, all TJ knew about the situation was sadness. He only knew that he was disappointing a lot of people. He was becoming increasingly depressed.

It was at this time that I learned of a therapeutic private school - The Logos School in Ladue, Missouri. I made an appointment to tour the school, and then drove my rickety car the thirty-minute trip over to the school.

When I walked into the small lobby of what was previously an abandoned elementary school, I sat down and waited for my tour guide. As I sat there, a very large and angry high school student walked into that small lobby.

It was just him and I. He was yelling and cussing, and he was angry. My first thought was, "Oh crap!". Then, I watched as three of the school staff walked up to him and began ***processing with him***. They did not ***react to him***. As I watched, I said to myself, "Yes! They just met that kid where he is at!". I desperately wanted TJ to have that same experience.

Then I toured the school and I fell in love with the place. They had a ratio of one licensed therapist for every eleven students. The students would do weekly individual therapy, and weekly group therapy. The staff also provided continuous real time processing with students throughout the day. Anytime something needed to be worked through, it was processed right there, sitting on the steps outside of the classroom.

I visited the financial office at the end of the tour. That is when I quickly returned to reality. Tuition was, at that time, twenty thousand per year, and here I was, a regular at the local food pantry.

As I drove back home, I was beating myself up. "Who do you think you are anyway? Visiting that rich people's school and wasting those peoples time?"

As I was driving, my cell phone rang. It was my ex-wife calling to tell me that TJ had been sent home from school. It was one of her days to have the kids. I asked, "Why did he get sent home?"

She told me that TJ said a cuss word.

I said, "Big deal".

She then added, and TJ will not stop talking about killing himself. He was eleven years old at the time.

I drove to her home to pick him up and take him out for an ice cream. As we were driving to the local McDonalds, TJ stared out the window and he said, "Dad?"

I said," Yes, what TJ?"

He said, "If I am dead, will my friends divide my toys?". Keep in mind that Autistic kids are lousy at contriving things. What you get is what is on their heart.

We had an ice cream and I felt like I had talked him into a better place, at least temporarily. Then I drove him back over to his mother's house.

I knew that there was no reason to believe things would get better with his current situation, and I was devastated.

When I got home, my mind went in circles. "I have to do something. But, financially, I don't have the ability to do anything!" Then, I stopped cold in my thoughts. I said to myself, "Money is not a good enough reason. Money is just not a good enough reason for TJ to not be in that school!"

With that, I sent an open email letter to my extended family, and to the extended family of my ex-wife. Essentially, I wrote, "If you have any philanthropic endeavors currently going on, I think that we have a project to consider that is very close to home".

My mother and my brother Olen stepped in with a great deal of financial help. I was also offered a significant scholarship from Logo's School on TJ's behalf. TJ attended Logos School for the next six years. It was a very good experience.

On a side note, I spoke to the behavior director at his public middle school before we made the move to Logos School. I told her about Logos School. I shared with her about the amazing therapeutic environment, and about the successful outcomes that troubled students were finding there. She seemed really excited.

To this point, I had been convinced that even though things were not going well in the public school, I had always believed that this behavior director was in my corner. I saw her as advocating as best as she possibly could on TJ's behalf.

So, I said to her, "I am glad that you are excited about this too! Will you consider recommending this program to be supported (financially) by the IEP Team/School District?" Before I could complete that sentence, she was already responding by saying, "Oh, God no!"

In that moment, it was clear to me that her response was not personal. It was a reflection of the school district's culture and priorities. My son was not one of those priorities.

I smiled at her, and I said nothing. From that moment on, I had clarity that she was advocating for something other than what was best for TJ. Her priority was the school district. She had been doing that all along, I just had not realized it until that moment.

After attending Logos School for six years, TJ wanted to graduate from his local public school. He left Logos School, and he did graduate from his public high school. From a social standpoint, however, the public high school was not a great experience for him.

His closest friends in the world, to this day are his buddies from Logos School.

TJ had a successful full-time work experience immediately following his high school graduation.

Six months later, he and I moved to Kansas City for a new job opportunity. This move would return me back to my original profession which is in manufacturing and consumer product sales to the mass retail trade channel.

From TJ's standpoint, he bounced between a few jobs that never lived up to what was promised. Then he worked in a grocery store for 2.5 years.

I became aware that he was deeply depressed, and that we needed a change. He and I relocated to Dallas, Texas in November of 2015. This move allowed him to participate in a technology and on-line game development program.

He was successful in that program, however, that program did not offer a legitimate path to a career and income. Last year, we moved to a new program where he works full time in a light manufacturing capacity.

He frequently drives back to St Louis and to Kansas City to spend time with friends. We plan to relocate to the St Louis area later this year so that TJ can be back with his lifelong friends on a more regular basis. He will also have similar work opportunities in the St. Louis area.

We are currently saving funds so that we can purchase rental properties. Our goal is to have eight or ten properties by the time that I retire.

TJ's greatest passion is in the buying and selling of American Classic Muscle Cars. He hopes to immerse himself in that business once we have established our real estate business.

Back in the year 1997, needless to say, the experts who predicted TJ's impending institutionalization were, quite wrong.

Simple History / Basic Facts

Chapter 4

A Short History of the Autism Diagnosis

Leo Kanner, an Austrian American psychiatrist is largely credited with publishing the original Autism Diagnosis in 1943. He was born in Austria, educated in Berlin, and he came to the United States in 1924.

Kanner established the First Children's Psychiatric Clinic in the United States at Johns Hopkins Hospital, Baltimore, MD in 1930.

Kanner's 1943 paper was titled, "Autistic Disturbances of Affective Contact". At that time, his diagnosis was largely on point. Kanner coined the term, infantile Autism, acknowledging that Autism was a condition largely present from birth.

Within that same paper, however, he also referred to at least one set of parents who he claimed had impacted the severity of their child as a result of their "cold parenting". This term that later evolved to be primarily referred to as "Refrigerator Mothers".

During this time within the medical community at large, there was a heavy Freudian influence. This Freudian influence suggested that most mental illness diagnosis could be attributed to some type of emotional injury early in life.

In the years that followed, Kanner moved further away from his initial findings that Autism occurs at birth.

In 1949, Kanner published a paper where he attributed the cause of Autism to be, "A genuine lack of parental warmth". Later, in a 1960 interview, Kanner bluntly described maternal parents of autistic children as having "Just happened to defrost enough to produce a child".

In 1969 Leo Kanner tried to walk back his comments, saying that he had been misquoted. He had not been misquoted. In his textbook, *Child Psychology*, revised in 1979, Kanner again supported the Refrigerator Parent theory.

Another big proponent for the Refrigerator Mother theory was a self-proclaimed psychologist, public intellectual and author.

His name was Bruno Bettelheim. He was a professor at the University of Chicago, and after 1973 he taught at Stanford University.

According to Wikipedia, "Bettelheim theorized that children with behavioral and emotional disorders were not born that way, and could be "cured" through extended psychoanalytic therapy, treatment that rejected the use of psychotropic drugs and shock therapy. During the 1960s and 1970s he had an international reputation in such fields as Autism, child psychiatry, and psychoanalysis. Much of his work was discredited after his death due to fraudulent academic credentials, allegations of abusive treatment of patients under his care, and accusations of plagiarism. Bettelheim's ideas, which grew out of Freud's, about alleged subconscious injury caused by mothers of troubled children are now seen as particularly damaging.

The University of Chicago was later criticized for not providing their normal oversight during Bettelheim's tenure. Chicago area psychiatrists were also later criticized for knowing at least some of what was occurring regarding the physical abuse of patients, and not taking effective action."

Bettelheim, in his 1967 book, *"Empty Fortress*: Infantile Autism and the Birth of

Self", compared Autism children "to being in a concentration camp". He went on to say, "Autism kids were never given a chance to develop a personality".

In case there were any doubts about his position, he further stated, "Autism is the product of mothers who were cold, distant and rejecting, thus depriving these children the chance to bond properly".

Hans Asperger, another prominent contributor to early Autism research, published his paper from within Nazi occupied Austria in 1944. Asperger reflected greater optimism about Autistic individuals. He was a proponent of a *spectrum* of Autism diagnosis. He also recognized the Autism diagnosis to be more widely present within the general population than Kanner.

Remarkably, Asperger's 1944 article was not translated into English until 1991. With that translation, Asperger's Syndrome was introduced into the Autism community as a classification to describe "high-functioning Autism".

While both Kanner and Asperger are recognized for important contributions towards the diagnosis and understanding of Autism, both have their detractors as well.

There is considerable evidence to suggest that Kanner was aware of Asperger's research, yet he was said to be desperate to be recognized for personal achievement in the medical community. With that, Kanner took all credit for the Autism Diagnosis discovery.

On his positives, Kanner was an early advocate for the mistreatment of mentally ill kids within state institutions. Kanner was also recognized for saving 200 doctors from Nazi death camps.

Asperger, on the other hand was believed to have been rewarded with advancement within the Nazi party for his cooperation after all Jewish doctors had been removed from Germany.

In addition, there is strong evidence to suggest that Asperger was on a committee that put to death thirty-five Autistic kids who were identified as "unteachable" kids. The Eugenics movement was alive and well in Nazi

Germany, as well as in the United States at that time. This is according to the following article, https://elderofziyon.blogspot.com/2018/05/the-truth-about-hans-asperger-nazi.html.

It is also remarkable to realize that the first Autism diagnosis reference did not appear in the DSM – The Diagnostic and Statistical Manual of Mental Disorders, until 1980!

Think about this. From approximately 1949 through 1960, the body of the medical establishment, all of those medical professionals in the white coats, blamed Autism almost exclusively on the theory of cold parenting! I cannot comprehend the level of guilt and devastation that those parents must have experienced.

Beyond the parental guilt, the other tragedy is that these kids were denied the help that they needed because the doctors were focused on false causes and therefore, false treatments.

Today, we know so much more. It is important to remember our history. With that knowledge and reflection, we are reminded of how easily dehumanizing belief systems can take hold when lazy thought is allowed to roam freely and unchallenged.

Today, even though we know so much more, and even though the Autism acceptance and awareness is so much better, the Autism conversation continues to exist within a We/They dynamic among society, generally speaking.

My mission with this book is to move the Autism conversation to an US dynamic within society. That is precisely where this conversation belongs.

This might all sound a bit like hair-splitting, but trust me, for those who live on the Autism Spectrum, this is anything but splitting hairs.

When we recognize the next better step to take in the Autism conversation, we should take it.

Why wouldn't we?

Chapter 5

Autism in Basic Terms

Autism is **sensory intensity difference**, that's it, nothing more, nothing less.

Taste, touch, smell, sound, sight, and I will add another one that I see as important within the Autism discussion. Thought.

The sensory experiences of an individual on the Autism spectrum can be 50 to 100 times as intense as those same sensory experiences for somebody who is not on the Autism Spectrum.

Imagine a sound, a distant screeching sound that you are hearing and experiencing at an intensity that is 50 times stronger than it is for those who are around you. This is a level of sound that actually exceeds a threshold of physical pain.

As an Autistic person, the associate that you are working along-side is probably not even registering that screeching sound. Yet for you, that sound is undeniable and overwhelming. Then, you might add to that situation, a faintly foul smell that is 70 times more intense for you, than for those around you. Then there may be florescent lighting that looks and sounds a lot like a repetitive laser.

You get the picture.

I am not suggesting that these sensory dynamics should be or could be fully understood by everybody.

I am advocating that we can acknowledge, without reservation, that every sensory experience is real and that every sensory experience is valid. No sensory experience is optional. This is true for you, this is true for me, this is true for everybody.

Within society, it seems sort of habitual for us to dismiss the unseen struggles of another person by attaching terms and descriptions that are derogatory in nature.

I sometimes wonder what a space alien would think when it observes human behavior.

That alien might think, "Why is it that, even though **every** *humanoid* has imperfections and anomalies, the larger group, the one that has more commonly experienced imperfections and anomalies, seems to place a greater level of value, relevance and "rightness" on their imperfections and anomalies?"

Why is one form of different more valid than another form of different?"

I think that Mr. Hypothetical Space Alien has a point.

Our habitual responses, and unfortunately a lot of existing language relative to Autism is long overdue for some updates in this regard.

I will go more into detail on the topic of outdated language in Chapter 14.

Chapter 6

One

I realize that the common messaging about Autism would lead you to believe that there are numerous, complex variations of Autism. This is actually not true.

Autism **is** *Sensory Intensity Difference*. That's it. Full Stop. Every Autism diagnosis lies on one continuum, there **are not** multiple forms of Autism.

There is One.

The term Spectrum can be confusing. When I first heard reference to the word, Spectrum, my initial response was to believe that there are a broad range of Autism types. Autism types that would each possess fundamentally unique characteristics.

The term Spectrum only serves to explain that some people with Autism have greater sensory intensity impacts, and some people with Autism have lesser sensory intensity impacts.

With this core element of truth, the next time that you encounter an individual on the Autism Spectrum, you can be confident that **you do know what you are looking at.** Be very assured on that. (*I will be offering additional facts to support this important understanding in the chapters that follow.*)

You can be confident that you understand the core elements of Autism. I am not saying that you should automatically *know* an Autistic individual on a personal level during a first encounter. Getting to know a person is a process, the same process that comes into play anytime you are getting to know any other person.

A message that exaggerates the complexity of Autism is self-defeating. It does not help anybody. The good news is, that message of complexity about Autism is quite wrong.

I'd like to share with you a simple, and accurate description of the Autism Spectrum Diagnosis.

According to the new DSM-5 (Diagnostic and Statistical Manual of Mental Disorders) published on January 1, 2014, there are three levels of Autism.

Level 1 Autism – Mild Sensory Intensity Impact

Level 2 Autism – Moderate Sensory Intensity Impact

Level 3 Autism – Significant Sensory Intensity Impact

Some might wonder, what about Asperger's Syndrome, isn't that another form of Autism?

No. Not anymore. The Asperger's Syndrome diagnosis was removed with the publication of DSM-5. Asperger's Syndrome is now classified within Level 1 Autism.

DSM-5(Stands for: Diagnostic and Statistical Manual of Mental Disorders) states that those who already had an Asperger's Syndrome diagnosis prior to the release of DSM-5 can still be recognized under their original diagnosis. A personal choice on that one I suppose. As of January 1, 2014, Asperger's Syndrome is no longer recognized as a newly diagnosed Autism Spectrum classification.

I think this might be a point in this book where some Neurologists, Psychologists, Counselors, Therapists, and other Trained Professionals might challenge the simplicity theme of my book.

Beyond the 3 levels of Autism noted above, there is some offshoot additional diagnosis nuances listed within DSM-5.

Let me just say this. To me, this is inside baseball stuff. I sometimes attend day long conferences and scribble out 30 pages of notes on new and interesting minutia related to the Autism conversation. Autism is my jam, and I get excited about this stuff like others might get excited about rock collecting.

My work background for many years has been in the area of product development, packaging, marketing and sales of consumer goods products to mass merchant retailers. In that world, we understand that if a product on a retail shelf captures the attention of a consumer for a fraction of a second, you get to score that as a big win.

Store shelves display an overwhelming assortment of products. As consumers, it can all become a blur.

The same is true about information. We are all overwhelmed with information. This is why I want to provide only the most succinct, core, fundamental information about Autism in this book. This is the information that you will retain, and this is the information that can permanently change what you think that you know about Autism, and how you interact with individuals on the Spectrum.

I can know you, embrace you and accept you without a requirement that I understand your physical and mental makeup in microscopic detail. That is all that I am saying here, about Autism.

Today, when we hear about an Autistic individual, a focus on this mystical, complex concept of Autism seems to take center stage while the humanity of the Autistic individual seems to take a back seat. This is what I am out to change. I am convinced that this change is very doable, and I truly believe that society is ready to embrace this change.

My hope in writing this book is not to train doctors, my hope in writing this book is to empower human connection.

When I meet somebody on the Autism Spectrum, I get excited. Sometimes, the person that I am speaking with may not even know and/or accept that they are on the Autism Spectrum. I had an experience like that recently.

To state the obvious, I am not qualified to diagnose anybody. I think my Autism radar is pretty good however, and when I see and hear idiosyncrasies that shout Autism, I operate on the assumption that I am interacting with somebody on the Spectrum.

Here is what happens when I encounter one of my people. I connect with them on the most human level possible. I go direct to that person's dignity. I get excited because, on some level, I suspect that I am connecting with them in a powerful and personal way that might not be so common.

The person that I am speaking to usually seems to come alive. The conversations take on an energy and life of their own. As those conversations come to an end, the energy of those individuals is always in a better place.

We all desire connection. Many on the Spectrum get used to that not happening. When I, or you, have confidence that we really do understand the core elements of Autism, we will also have confidence in our ability to connect with individuals who on the Spectrum.

Everybody wants that. Everybody wins when that happens. That is what this book is all about.

Chapter 7

Experts are - Human

There has been high-level resistance to the DSM-5 initiatives that advocate straight talk and simplicity over complexity about the Autism Spectrum diagnosis.

Dr. Fred Volkmer, Director of the Yale Child Study Center, co-authored a paper in 2012, shortly before the new DSM-5 was released. This Yale professor complained a great deal about the new streamlined and simplified DSM-5 criteria for the Autism diagnosis.

In an article published in a Yale School of Medicine newsletter on April 10, 2012, he stated that his research revealed, that as a result of the updated criteria contained in DSM-5, 25% of individuals on the Autism Spectrum would no longer qualify for an Autism diagnosis. He also said that his research showed that a staggering 75% of those diagnosed as Asperger's Syndrome would no longer qualify for an Autism diagnosis.

A peer review of Mr. Volkmer's article found that only 4% of those diagnosed with Asperger's Syndrome _might_ have an altered diagnosis under the new DSM-5 criteria.

Dr. Volkmer has not let up on his affinity for complexity. In May of 2018, he co-authored an article with Brian Reichow (Assoc. Prof at University of Florida). That article was published in SectrumNews.org.

In that article, Volkmer and Reichow complained that prior to DSM-5, they had more than 2000 combinations of criteria that could be blended to establish an Autism diagnosis. With the introduction of DSM-5, Volkmer and Reichow lament that there are now only 12 combinations of criteria that can lead to an Autism diagnosis.

I am personally a lot more comfortable with the idea that I can be adequately known and understood and embraced through 12 combinations of criteria. Promoting the idea that my identity can only be narrowed down and understood to be 1 within 2000 is really just another way of saying that I can never be truly embraced, understood and accepted.

From a perspective of skeletal, muscular and cellular characteristics, I am sure that it could be said that we all possess 2000(probably a lot more) unique, individual differences. It is just that it would be unfair, even de-humanizing to say that I cannot know you, accept you and embrace you until I have a working understanding of each of the 1000's of unique skeletal, muscular and cellular characteristics of your body.

I don't need to know anywhere near that level of microscopic detail about you in order to fully embrace your humanity.

Speaking as a human being from behind the eyes of Autism, we are just not that complicated. No more complicated than you.

I have some sensory intensities that are different than the ones that you have. And, you have many personality and sensory attributes that are different than the ones that I have.

We really are all humans swimming around in the same sea of humanity. Not a "We" sea, not a "They" sea, but truly an "US" sea.

All people are human, even the most educated ones. Sometimes we get it right, sometimes we get it wrong. No exceptions on that.

A final thought, Parents, you know your kids. Psychiatrists, psychologists, neurologists and counselors can help you better understand important nuances that define your kids.

You are the boss, and for a very good reason. Of course, the best bosses are teachable bosses, but they're still the boss.

We should never forget that.

Chapter 8

You *Can* See It

I spoke to Temple Grandin at a conference in Addison, Texas on September of 2018. We also spoke at another conference in Irving, Texas in September of 2019.

For those who might not be familiar with Temple Grandin, she became the first highly public figure who has been significantly impacted and diagnosed on the Autism Spectrum.

Temple was born in 1947, only four years after the original Autism diagnosis was published. To say that there was zero understanding of the Autism diagnosis within society at the time of her birth is an understatement.

Temple's mother was really on point with her instincts about how to both accept and also to embrace Temple for who she is. She would nudge Temple to try new things, to push her slightly beyond her comfort zones.

Temple was non-verbal until the age of four. She spent a lot of time in her childhood on a farm. Among other things, Temple was fascinated with the animals, and with farming operations in general.

She recognized that the squeezers that hold the cattle during the milking process were also really effective for reducing her stress associated with Autism sensory overload. She would get in the squeezer machine and the deep pressure experience would provide a powerful calming sensation. Temple redesigned the cattle squeezers to better fit people. Based on her discovery, deep pressure and weighted blankets are a type of therapy which is widely implemented today.

Temple's high school science teacher noticed her fascination with beef cattle farming. He made it possible for her to spend time each week at a local cattle/beef processing operation.

Temple had a strong sense about what stressed the animals. With that in mind, she created an entirely new design concept for cattle handling facilities.

Temple's design replaced the hard-angled cattle chutes with rounded and flowing chutes. She got down on her hands and knees and crawled through the chutes to mimic the experience from a cow's perspective. She made note of every element in her direct or peripheral vision that might startle or spook an animal, and she made changes where they were needed.

Though untrained in architectural drawing, Temple created remarkably detailed, perfect to scale, hand drawn architectural renderings for her new concept cattle handling facilities.

As a result, today in America, more than half of the cattle processing facilities that exist have been designed by Temple. She has also been called upon by many international companies to re-design their cattle handling facilities as well.

Temple's story is remarkable, and many great books have been written to chronicle her story in detail. Temple has personally written 87 books to date.

Keeping to the purpose of this book, simplicity, I am focusing on core basics that support a powerful fact: Temple's story is one that illustrates, **you can see autism**, in the brain. You can look at it!

This is possible thanks to a technological advancement called Functional MRI technology. (Realtime MRI)

In Temple Grandin's book, "The Autistic Brain", published in 2014, she references the series of MRI's that have been conducted on her brain over the years by several research organizations.

For a long time, these MRI studies were based on the traditional, Static MRI process. With the advent of Functional MRI, we can now observe the synapse fire within specific sensory processing regions of the brain.

The differences are highly apparent. This visual evidence creates remarkable distinctions that are measured when comparing, side by side Functional MRI images.

According to Temple's book, The Autistic Brain, "Within the FMRI imaging for Temple Grandin, you can see that her visual tract is

400% overdeveloped when compared to a control subject(non-autistic brain fMRI)."

The visual tract area of the brain is highly involved in tasks such as architectural rendering. This would support her surprising ability to create precise and detailed architectural renderings without having been trained to do so.

Temple's book also notes, "You can also see that the "say what you see" connection within her auditory system is only at 1% of development when compared to that of the control subject. As a result of this difference, Temple experienced difficulty in speaking as a child that was similar to stuttering."

There are differences found in other sensory processing regions of Temple's brain, but these two differences were the most striking.

Temple's book, "The Autistic Brain" also stressed, "It is important to note that the neuroimaging provided by fMRI does not provide the same precise image each time the brain is scanned."

In other words, fMRI does not take a 3-D image of the brain that can reveal in a snap-shot view, areas within the Autistic brain that have enhanced or diminished sensory processing development.

When neurons fire within a specific area of the brain, it looks a lot like a lightning storm. There is a glow, then the area lights up with brightness, and then it fades out." This is what the fMRI will show.

The fMRI can only observe brain responses while a person lies as still as possible. While the fMRI does not capture the brains full range of activity, it does provide physical and tangible evidence that Autism is present, physiologically, within the brain.

I stress this point because I have talked to many parents who, on some level, deny or to diminish the idea that their child is exhibiting behaviors suggesting the presence of Autism.

If you can look at it, and if you can see it, then when Autism is present, denial is truly not an option. Parents should investigate first. If it is not there, then nothing is lost.

Chapter 9

Common Sound Experiences

I have been offering some general examples about the impacts of sounds and noises on Autistic individuals. See specific listing below:

Note-Individuals on the Spectrum can experience these same sounds at 50 to 100 times greater intensity.

130db – Jet engine at 100 ft.

120db – Thunder (*Threshold of physical pain*)

110 db – Rock Music, Screaming Child.

90 db – Factory Machinery at 3 ft.

80 db – Busy Street, Alarm Clock

70 db – Busy Traffic, Phone Ringtone

60 db – Normal Conversation at 3 ft.

50 db – Quiet Office, Quiet Street

40 db – Quiet Residential Park

30 db – Quiet Whisper at 3 ft., Library

20 db – Rustling Leaves, Ticking Watch

These sound measurements can be found in SpectrumNews.org and Restoredhearing.com.

Many individuals on the Autism Spectrum describe audible sensory overwhelm in terms of a physical, stabbing pain. As you can see by the chart, 120db for a normal hearing range sensitivity marks a threshold of physical pain.

For individuals on the Autism Spectrum, a 120db or greater sound experience/threshold of pain is possible within ANY of these sound reference examples.

I am not sharing this sort of information to guilt anybody. I share this information to explain sound experiences might be impacting Autistic individuals around you.

For an individual on the spectrum, sensory layering is also a very real thing. For people who know me closely, we joke sometimes about "Morning Tony" and "Evening Tony".

Morning Tony is very present, in the moment. Evening Tony is "still in the house", but he is definitely different. Sensory experiences throughout my day layer upon each other. In order to fully connect in the evenings, I have a lot more sensory residue (for lack of a better word) to work through.

This is basic and logical. Sensory stuff stacks up during the day. A good nap or a good night's sleep will wipe the slate clean.

This may be different, but again, it is really not complicated.

Humanity

Chapter 10

Cure V/S Acceptance

My process in writing this book has really been a scramble. Since I resigned my full-time job, I have been scratching out my needed funding by driving uber about 60 hours per week. I also deal with the daily menu of family issues that come up, just like we all do.

My schedule has only allowed for about 20 hours a week to write, so the process of completing this book has taken longer than I had expected.

There have been some important benefits that have come along with my extended timeline. For one thing, I have had a number of meaningful conversations while working that have helped me gain greater insight.

Sometimes, these conversations have resulted in new chapters that I had not planned.

Recently I was talking with a young lady who had just relocated from Chicago, to North Dallas. We were talking about some of my long-term issues with the Autism Spectrum "Cure Movement".

I have always had big problems with the Cure Movement. I expected this young lady to nod her head along in agreement as I was talking, but that is not what happened. Instead, she told me, "Actually, I think there is a very strong case to be made for the Cure Movement".

She went on to tell me about a close friend who has a child that is Level 3 Autistic. This child will never be independent, and this child will always require intensive supports. Wouldn't it be better if this child, and this family, had a different life?

To be honest, this issue has haunted me throughout the process of writing this book. I have nibbled at this question and I have picked at the edges of this conflict, but this topic was still bothering me a lot.

In response to her challenge, I dug in my heels and I talked about the inherent and precious value of every life. I went on about how planet earth, in my view, is infinitely better because of the existence of every one of these precious souls, without exception. I was offering everything I had to offer to make my case, but she did not budge.

She told me, "I get all of that, but, again, wouldn't advances in science and medicine be a good thing? Wouldn't it be better if my friend's son had the chance to live a full and complete life just like most other kids?"

I tried to find more convincing points to argue, but I could tell that I was losing steam. I am so driven by the humanity element of this conversation that I honestly cannot entertain even a hint of, "What if this person impacted by Autism had not been impacted by Autism?".

I realize that this probably sounds irrational, but I am so connected to the acceptance of the individual, right here and right now, in this moment, that to even allow for that question opens a line of reasoning that breaks my heart. It just does.

I have encountered many people who talk about their Autistic child in way that say's "We need to fix him or her, we just do!". The same time they are saying that, the body language and voice inflection is telling a different story. "I can't fix him (or her) and that's never going to be ok!". And that...... breaks my heart. I hear it all the time, I really do. That lack of acceptance, to me, is tragic.

While I was debating this young lady from Chicago, I was thinking, "This is something that I cannot budge on!"

Then, right before my brain exploded, I realized that my only real option in this debate was to surrender. My surrender that was only made possible because of her equally impassioned argument.

Here is where I landed in my thinking. Above all else, I trust God's plan. If it is within God's plan that Autism be eradicated from life as we know it, then I trust that God is taking us to a better place.

Mind you, this better place is one that I cannot imagine. Life as we know it, here and now, on planet Earth is one that would be massively diminished, in my view, without the immeasurable impact of Autistic individuals, both practically and spiritually, throughout history and up to this moment.

With that, I acknowledge that medical advancement and even a cure, if that were to happen according to God's good and perfect plan, would be a good thing. Probably better than I can imagine.

My bottom line is this, Cure people, you go and do your Cure thing. Good luck with that. Seriously.

My focus will continue to be about acceptance. I will appreciate every good development that research can provide, as long as it places acceptance and humanity of the individual, right here, right now as its highest priority.

For me, this debate was a gift. I have better clarity today that my personal mission is solely and completely focused on the humanity of the Autistic individual.

Chapter 11

Knock-Knock, Who IS in there?

Me

Me who?

Me - Me! Who else did you think would be in here?

I'd like to share a life story that illustrates the point of this chapter. There is some background here, so stay with me on this ok?

When my son TJ was originally diagnosed on the Spectrum, I attended several parent support-groups. These were groups that typically involved about ten moms, and a dude. Me.

I also became part of an organization called The National Association of Autism Research (N.A.A.R.). This was a national organization which was formed in 1994. It is an organization that stressed both acceptance of Autism and Autism research. I supported these ideals, especially the acceptance part, so I was eager to join in and support this organization.

The local, St. Louis Missouri N.A.A.R. chapter was primarily there to organize and to manage a large fundraiser walk that would take place in Forest Park every summer. The annual fundraiser walks were well attended and highly successful in raising money for research.

A new Autism advocacy group known as *Autism Speaks was formed in February of 1995. Autism Speaks was celebrity driven, and as a result, Autism Speaks had high visibility and strong financial support.

At the time of its formation, and for many years after, Autism Speaks was largely focused on the idea of **curing** Autism.

This obsession with cure made me uncomfortable. I would say to people at that time, "Don't talk to me about cure. My boy is here. I don't need to fix him. I don't need to trade him in. I don't need to make him ok. He is ok. In fact, he is perfect! I need to **know** him, that is what I need! When I know him, when I fully understand him, then we can go anywhere that we can go, together!"

I can't fully explain why the mindset of cure so repelled me, but it did. I have since spoken to many who are on the Autism Spectrum, who share that sentiment. For many on the Spectrum, the word cure is closely related to the term eradication, and eradication is a term closely related to the term eugenics.

In 1996, Autism Speaks and NAAR decided to merge because they felt that their combined resources and experience would benefit the agendas of research, acceptance, and cure. Within this new arrangement, Autism Speaks was positioned as the parent umbrella entity of that merger.

I immediately said, "I'm out! I won't have any part of this." I felt like I was being a jerk, but I couldn't help myself, I just really could not stomach being a part of it.

Stay with me here, ok? I have not forgotten the title of this chapter. We are getting there, I promise!

I began searching on the internet to find other individuals or organizations that shared my stubborn mindset on the cure issue. Then I found an on-line organization based in NYC called GRASP.

GRASP is short for Global and Regional Aspergers Syndrome Partnership. It has long been the largest support organization created and run by adults who are on the Autism Spectrum.

The leader of the organization was a guy named Michael Jon Carley. He was a Broadway playwright among other things, and his son was diagnosed on the spectrum in late 2000. Michael himself was then diagnosed one week later.

The thing that compelled me most when I read about this organization online was their mission statement. It was radical at the time. To paraphrase, it said something to the effect of, "Stop trying to cure us. We're not sick!"

I called Michael and I was so relieved to be speaking directly to somebody else who shared my stubborn views on this topic. We had a nice conversation, one that I greatly appreciated.

GRASP was also looking to add chapters across the country. I was interested in establishing a chapter in the St. Louis, MO region. Reality intervened with my plan, however. At that time, I was hardly able to work because I was at school almost every day dealing with teacher and staff issues. I had no bandwidth to take on that sort of endeavor.

Now, on to the original point of this chapter, thanks for staying with me.

One of the writers on the GRASP web site was a girl named Amanda. Amanda had been so impacted by her Autism sensory intensity experience early in life that throughout her childhood and adolescence she would enjoy life mostly through stemming, in a corner, alone.

Many people doubted her intellectual capacity as she was growing up. As a young adult writer, however, Amanda was not only technically excellent, she was also connecting on every level of emotion with her writing. In other words, although many, many people perceived through external impressions that there was essentially "nobody home", there had always been a whole and complete person in front of them. People were distracted or confused by her external ticks and gestures, and they just didn't see the whole and complete person behind the Autism ticks.

As is always the case with individuals on the Autism Spectrum, there is within Amanda, a 100% whole and complete person, emotionally, intellectually, spiritually, on every level and in every way.

There is a simple truth that you can take away from her story. Whenever you are present with an individual who is diagnosed on the Autism Spectrum, no matter how significantly they are impacted by their Autism, you can always be certain that you are interacting with a whole and complete person, spiritually, intellectually, and emotionally. This is always true and there are no exceptions.

Since this is ALWAYS true, this affirms a very powerful, simple truth about Autism.

You never have to wonder who is in front of you. When you encounter an individual on the Autism Spectrum, that person in front of you is, **YOU.**

Even when there are no obvious indications or apparent awareness of social connection, this will always be true.

I encourage you to speak with confidence to the humanity of the whole and complete person. You will never go wrong in doing so.

Autism Speaks officially removed the word cure from their mission statement and from all organizational media in September of 2014. Good on them for doing so.

Chapter 12

Be Right There

When TJ was in public elementary school, and even half-way into his sixth-grade middle school, many of the staff who worked with him would complain that he simply would not follow direction.

Each time that I would hear this, I would think, "How are time-prompts working in this situation?" *(Time prompts are basically ques that allow an Autistic individual, deep in thought, needed time to transition back to focus on the here and now.)*

My question about time prompts would seemingly to fall on deaf ears.

Looking back, I realize that I should have been more emphatic and relentless on this issue. For me, it was instinct to think ahead and prepare TJ for upcoming changes. During those days, I just didn't fully embrace how critical the issue of time prompts was and is for TJ.

This really is simple stuff. While they were failing to get TJ to transition, I was having none of those problems.

I would give TJ a heads-up, usually a 10-minute notice, a follow up at 5 minutes, and then a final follow up at 1 minute. Something like this:

"Hey T, in about 10 minutes, were gonna need to leave for school. "

"Hey T, were gonna be rolling in about 5".

"Hey T, were gonna leave in about a minute".

A minute later, it would be, and still is, essentially an automatic response for TJ to be ready to roll.

Why?

Keep in mind that an individual on the Autism Spectrum has sensory intensity experiences that can be 50 to 100 times greater than those same sensory experiences for an individual who is not on the Autism Spectrum.

Thought is not actually a sense, but, from many personal experiences working with my son and with others on the spectrum, I believe that the intensity of **thought** can also be 50 to 100 times greater. This is entirely logical.

An individual who is not on the Spectrum might be thinking a certain thought, and then may wander two or three corridors into connecting thoughts.

In that same vein, an individual on the Autism Spectrum may start with one thought and then go ten, twenty or fifty corridors deeper into related or connecting thoughts.

When we accept and embrace this intensity of thought element, then we can understand that to walk up to an individual on the Spectrum, and out of the blue say, stop doing "this", now do "that!", it is understandable why instant transitions are almost always the wrong approach.

To put it another way, often the individual on the spectrum is not actually **"here"**, he or she is actually **"there"**, deep into a chain of connecting thoughts. He or she is willing to return to **"here"**, but from a practical consideration, this is a journey that will take some time. This explains why surprises usually do not go well for individuals on the spectrum.

This example illustrates why time prompting works really well.

There is, as Einstein and others would attest, great benefit that can come from this intensity of thought, we just need to embrace how best to support it.

Time prompting is a great, simple tool which makes it possible for your company to support highly talented, loyal and productive employees who are on the Autism Spectrum.

Chapter 13

Agitated or Busy?

As I already noted, the sensory experience of an individual on the Autism Spectrum can much more intense than normal.

With that in mind, I ask you to imagine that you are sitting in a classroom. It is just another day for most of the kids in that class. The instructor has assigned a short story writing project. The students are generally engaged in their writing. Nothing seemingly out of the ordinary here.

There is a construction project one block down the street from the school. A new convenience store will be open within a month or two.

The distant drone of diesel engine noise is audible, but not really noticeable for most of the kids. The machinery emits muted, distant sounds of screeching and clicking from the metal bull-dozer tracks.

You are sitting at your desk, but you are not getting your work done. You really want to get your work done. You really like it when the instructor smiles at you with approval for your assignments that have been completed.

You, of course, are Autistic.

The other kids can stop and think about that those construction noises if they decided to go there. The other kids filter out those sounds and noises because they are mild and distant. The other kids can focus on the assignment so that they can get it completed.

You don't hear a distant rumble of machinery, or the muted clicking and screeching sounds. You hear those noises at an intensity level that is shocking to your system.

Your head is throbbing. Fight, flight or freeze instincts pull at you. You don't want to stand out from the other kids, so you are hanging on by your fingernails.

You try to write, but the calamity is relentless. This is very frustrating. To the casual observer, it can be easy to conclude that you are agitated. But think about it.

You are not agitated. You are busy!

This is a truth that should always be respected. This truth should always be honored.

Nobody in that classroom is trying harder or working with a greater intensity than you are to get that assignment completed without causing a distraction.

Your effort is not worthy of derogatory or dismissive words like agitated, but all too easily, we can attach these sorts of labels to individuals who are on the Spectrum when we don't understand what we are seeing.

In this scenario, you may be showing no obvious or apparent awareness of the disapproval that is coming from your peers or instructors, but you know.

You are unable to quantify and explain your feelings, but you comprehend at a deep level that you are disappointing the people around you. You feel less than, that you are not enough, that you are the problem.

I am not sharing this scenario to elicit guilt, to convict or to accuse. Never, on any level will I do that.

This is insight shared in order to enlighten you. Now you know. Now you know what to do.

Autism Sensory Intensities are legit. There is no mystery here. Makes sense, right?

Chapter 14

Another Take on This

In this classroom scenario, you are not aware that the other kids **are not** battling the same sensory intensity distractions that you are battling.

I can attest that as an individual on the Spectrum, the first person who I have blamed for my social awkwardness and/or miscues has always been me.

Since, you, the Autistic person behind those elevated sensory intensity experiences is a whole, complete, complex human being, you experience every emotion, fear or insecurity that others do. Those emotions are often experienced at a much greater intensity.

By the time that I was in my late teens, I had concluded that I was the lowest life form on earth, and I was certain that the world would be a better place without me.

According to a study posted in a recent Psychology Today article, The Link between

Suicide and Autism, "Individuals on the Autism Spectrum are 66% more likely to have suicidal ideation, and 34% more likely to plan out or to attempt suicide."

I mention this in relation to this hypothetical classroom story for an obvious reason. This stuff really does matter a great deal.

Chapter 15

Language

In this chapter, I point out some psychological and therapy related language that I truly believe should change. Do I actually believe that these changes will happen in the near future, if ever? Doubtful.

Again, I am giving voice and putting words to issues from a perspective that is behind the eyes of Autism. Many of these issues go unchallenged by individuals on the Spectrum because, well, why bother? It is just easier to surrender to the mob on stuff like this. "Society is like a freight train, roaring down the track. My little protest is not going to slow it down".

If that is the reality about this topic, then, what's the point? First of all, I think I am right, so I ought to talk about it. Secondly, my mission is to reach hearts and minds through my book, and through my public speaking.

I hope that you will embrace and internalize what I am sharing. For you, and for the individuals on the Autism Spectrum that you will encounter, this information will impact lives for the better, one person at a time.

And who knows, maybe one of us will at some point encounter people of influence within the medical community who care about this stuff. One can always hope.

My focus is on the humanity of the Autistic individual. On that level, this conversation matters.

If any language diminishes rather than uplifts, I say there are no mulligans. If language can be made better, then it should be made better. Over the centuries, a lot of unacceptable language has been changed, and for good reason. Occasional reflection on the language that we choose is a good thing.

I will begin with somebody familiar, Dr. Leo Kanner, for some reference and context. While studying the life history and the professional history of Dr. Kanner, the publisher of the first Autism diagnosis, I came across medical language that was mainstream in the 1940's that is no longer acceptable today. Somethings do change for the better, over time, at a societal level.

Mr. Kanner's groundbreaking research provided great steps forward in identifying and publishing the first Autism Spectrum diagnosis in 1943. Most of his contributions to the field of psychology actually took place from the early 1930's through the mid 1940's.

While Kanner was the first to name the Autism Syndrome condition, and to define and publish research on the Autism Diagnosis, Kanner also wrote papers during this era about topics that included **morons** and **imbeciles**. Kanner participated in debates regarding the euthanizing of **idiots** in 1942. For the record, Kanner was on the *"against"* euthanizing side of that argument, but at the time, he was comfortable with that language.

In fairness, those were and are psychological terms. That noted, there are very good reasons why those terms are no longer commonly used within the practice of psychology.

One example of Kanner's published works centered on discerning the practical

usefulness of idiots to society-(garbage collection, cotton pickers, oyster shuckers).

http://www.brown.uk.com/teaching/HEST5001/joseph.pdf

It can be easy to judge psychological language and methodology used during 1940's America as cold and barbaric. It is fair to acknowledge that prevailing understandings within the psychology field during the 1940's were a work in progress. This should always the case.

Today, we have greater knowledge and better understanding. Positive changes in the use of that old language has happened as a result.

For further context on those terms, according to Wikipedia, "Moron is a term once used in psychology and psychiatry to denote mild intellectual disability. The term was closely tied with the American Eugenics Movement. Once the term became popularized as a disparaging epithet, it fell out of use by the psychological community. It is similar to imbecile and idiot."

According to the Wordnik app from the American Heritage Dictionary, "Imbecile is a person who is considered foolish or stupid, and a person of moderate to severe mental retardation having a mental age of from three to seven years, and generally being capable of some degree of communication and performance of simple tasks under supervision. The term belongs to a classification system no longer in use and is now considered offensive.

According to Wikipedia, an idiot is a stupid or foolish person. It was formerly a technical term in legal and psychiatric contexts for some kinds of profound intellectual disability where the mental age is two years or less, and the person cannot guard himself or herself against common physical dangers.

Again, these words were established as psychological terms that later took on derogatory and diminishing meaning within popular culture.

These terms have not fallen out of favor simply because they sound bad. They have also fallen out of favor because they often have dark, sinister or dehumanizing associations.

According to timetoast.com, Modern Psychology was born on January 1, 1775. A **lot** has changed for the better since 1775.

Following are some terms and phrases that come to mind that I hope to see updated sooner rather than later. Accuracy and context matter and these are some phrases that I believe miss the mark knowing what we know today.

1) Autism Spectrum Disorder

Autism Spectrum is a straightforward, fact-based identifier for the Autism condition that is both accurate **and** without derogatory inference.

I have no issue with the diagnosis name, Autism Spectrum. It actually confuses me when some people are bothered when being accurately described as **Autistic.**

Autistic refers to an individual that has brain development, specifically sensory intensity processing differences, that are consistent with the **Autism Spectrum** identifier.

I don't see anything in that name that is derogatory. If one is disturbed by the use of the word **Autistic**, doesn't that actually suggest that there is something *wrong* with people who are Autistic? Different and bad are two different things, and we on the Spectrum are good with being who we are. It is all that we know. It is our best life experience.

Disorder... Ok, here is where my problem comes in. I believe that the use of the word Disorder in this instance is both demeaning and inaccurate. When you think about it, exactly what **"order"** is measured against this **"dis-order"**? Who is this inferred person of comparison who is without blemish, without anomaly, without imperfection?

Count me definitely in the camp of being against this continued use of the word disorder. It is just a lazy and derogatory word, I don't care how many really smart people want to defend it.

I think that it should be replaced with:

Range of Sensory Intensity Impact

Range of Sensory Intensity Impact is a description that is accurate on every level.

And, there is nothing demeaning or derogatory about this description.

For what it is worth, I believe that the term Disorder should be eliminated as a psychological term for every diagnosis. I vote for fewer inaccurate nicknames and for more accurate descriptions please.

Some might ask, "Do individuals on the Autism Spectrum really care about this use of the term, disorder?"

I believe that this is the wrong question. The relevant question is, "Do individuals living on the Autism Spectrum *feel* the impact of a word like disorder? Yes. We do. And this is completely unnecessary.

If the word disorder is a fixed portion of my identity, then I am disordered. Then I am less, and you are more. Then I am messed up, and you are put together. Then I am a problem, or an interruption in the *normal* flow of life, and you are not.

If I am "disordered", then I am *they* and you are *we*. We can do better, and we should.

2) Intervention:

When we first received my son's diagnosis, the only thing that I felt sure of was that I was not really sure of anything.

Thoughts and images of what life with Autism might look like, and might feel like, flooded my mind.

Then, right away, somebody started talking to me about something called **Intervention!**

That term, Intervention, felt and sounded to me like a mission to hunt down, identify, target, destroy, eviscerate, and eliminate this thing called Autism.

The problem with that is that Autism exists in my son's brain. It is physiological. It is there.

I don't want to destroy Autism. I want to *know* it! I want to know everything about it. I want to know what it likes. I want to know what it doesn't like. I want to know how I can tap into, accept and embrace this incredible and unique brain. I want to meet Autism and shake hands with it, that's what I want to do.

I am not suggesting that Autism programs designed to understand and to support abilities, gifts, talents and passions of Autistic individuals are bad things.

When you think about it, those programs sound a lot like college. Autism programs and college courses can enhance what is already good, teaching rather than intervening.

So, if not intervention, then what?

I would be a lot more comfortable with

Life Skills Planning.

It is better. Better is better than worse. It should happen. This is not complicated.

3) Trigger:

I believe that the word Trigger, as used in this context to describe a cause for Autism Spectrum sensory overwhelm is inflammatory and demeaning.

The word "trigger" hyper focuses on the *result* of a sensory layering or overwhelming circumstance, while at the same time the word Trigger invalidates or ignores the actual cause.

Trigger, just another lazy nickname that distorts and confuses. *"Better walk on eggshells around that guy, I don't want to TRIGGER him!"*

Wouldn't it be better if we committed ourselves to tracking down, understanding *and embracing* the sensory reality experiences that are making an Autistic individual uncomfortable? Wouldn't that be better than tossing out a dismissive nickname that only serves to feed confusion?

I don't have a suggested replacement word or phrase for "trigger". I say, just don't go there.

Go to a better place instead.

4) **Meltdown**:

Meltdown is another nickname that is commonly projected on Autistic individuals who are experiencing sensory stimulation to a degree that is overwhelming and/or painful.

Meltdown, I believe, is a word that only serves to blame an individual on the Autism Spectrum for having a legitimate awareness of their sensory reality experience. How does that make sense?

Like the term Trigger, I have no replacement to suggest for the term Meltdown. I think that Meltdown is yet another nickname that should just be retired.

When we dispense of the lazy nicknames, then we are forced to focus on facts instead. Nicknames may be easier, but relevant truth delivers profoundly better outcomes.

I am sure that there are other terms and phrases in need of refinement, replacement or retirement. When we honor the sensory reality experiences of individuals on the Spectrum as our highest motivation, then we will dispense of lazy language.

My sincere hope is that we will continue to grow, and that we will continue to do better in the area of language relative to the Autism Spectrum diagnosis.

Chapter 16

Need to be Right

There is a standard saying around an alcoholism recovery program, "If you spot it, you got it!"

In other words, I see an excessive need in others to be right because I have an excessive need to be right.

My need to be right is so pronounced in fact, that early in my recovery, my sponsor realized that I "qualify" for more than just a 12-step program for sobriety. He assigned me a second program as well. This one is a 5-Step recovery program to address my over-functioning need to be right. It goes something like this:

1) I have a need to be right about this.
2) I am willing to be wrong about this.
3) Here is what I think about this.
4) What do you think about this?
5) Then, my most difficult step – I listen to you. I hear you. I evaluate your point of view. I earnestly search to see where you might be right and where I might be wrong.

When I speak to Autism parents, family and friends of Autism Individuals, I sometimes think others could benefit from this program too.

I seem to have a knee jerk reaction as my first instinct when people introduce me a new type of thought or approach about Autism. I think it is just scary for me to think that I might be doing something that is less than the very best for my son.

I have to work through that feeling, to admit my need to be right, and to expose myself to the risk being wrong

I share this because I often speak to parents, friends, families and acquaintances of individuals on the Autism Spectrum who, like me, need to believe that they have it figured out, that they are right, doing the best that can possibly be done.

I spoke to one man recently, an affluent guy who began to describe his son to me. He described traits and characteristics about his son that shouted Autism. He also shared with me that his son had not yet been diagnosed.

I just got excited for him and I encouraged him, "Grab this thing by the horns! There is such good news in front of you! You just need to get some professional insight on this awesome and unique individual who is your son. With good information, you will understand, fully understand and fully embrace your son for who he truly is.

He already knows who he is relative to his Autistic world view and experience. He cannot wait for you to join with him on this journey! What are you waiting for?"

I did not say all of that, word for word, but those were the sentiments that I was hoping I could get across to that father.

It was at this point in the conversation that he said to me, "You know what, my son is actually doing pretty well without all of that diagnosis stuff. I think we are going to just keep doing what we are doing. We will just continue to work through this.".

That sort of a response breaks my heart. When you look at a Functional MRI, and you see the clear physical evidence of Autism existing in the brain, you understand that "working through this" is not actually an option for that boy.

That boy will probably pretend to be something other than who he really is, as best as he can, in order to please his father. In other words, he will deny himself. In doing so, he will, on some level internalize a belief that he is not enough.

As for the father, this is more than just a denial. Given what we know about the physical presence of Autism, this is actually rejection. I realize that is a hard statement, but as one who is speaking from behind the eyes of Autism, there is just no other way to say it.

Of course, I know that this Dad loves his son and that he wants to do anything that he can to support him.

I just hope that dad will think about what we talked about, and that he will get beyond his, quite understandable, need to be right on this.

Chapter 17

Dig for the Diamond

What do I mean by digging for diamonds? I mean, cut loose! I mean, radically dismiss expectations, radically dismiss societal "norms", radically dismiss "the way things ought to be", radically dismiss "average"!

I mean, stop planet earth and spin it backwards!

When I say, dig for that diamond, I mean if you have the slightest hunch that your kid, significant other, husband, wife, relative, or any common acquaintance might be on the Autism Spectrum, do not retreat. Get excited instead and lean into it with fascination and with anticipation.

Run to it. Run to it with every ounce of energy that you possess.

Why such an impassioned plea? Two important reasons come immediately to mind. I believe that society continually whispers to us that the most common way is the preferred way. The right way.

I think that this pull to assimilate, to be seen as leading the (normal) pack, is really strong. I don't have science to back up this statement, I can only say that this is a strong hunch for me personally.

For most of us, I believe it matters, probably a little bit too much, what parents, friends, associates and peers, pretty much anybody, thinks about us. Some more than others. It is probably more accurate to say, it matters a great deal what we *think* that others are thinking about us.

I initially allowed those influences to inhibit my willingness and my commitment to fully embrace my son's Autism. I eventually got there. I just wish that I had arrived sooner. My son deserved that. Every kid deserves that.

I don't want to dismiss the process that might be the seven stages of grief, I just hope to help shorten that process a great deal for future parents, siblings, friends and peers who will encounter a new Autism Spectrum diagnosis.

Your kid is already there, living out his or her Autism Spectrum life experience. He or she can't wait for you to join in, **all in** on an amazing adventure.

Whether it be societal influences or personal expectations, I see many parents who caveat their acceptance of an Autism Spectrum diagnosis. Many never fully buy-in, to accept and to embrace.

I will close this chapter by again encouraging each of us to always dig for that diamond.

Even if we find that an Autism hunch is wrong, we will reveal in greater clarity, the spectacular diamond that is our child, better understood, better accepted and better known for who he or she is.

Essentially, it is impossible to go wrong here.

No reason for hesitation.

Just Dig!

Chapter 18

"I Am So Sorry?"

Over the years I have had many people say to me, "I am so sorry", when we are discussing Autism and its impacts on my life journey and that of my family.

I realize that these people are just searching for something supportive and kind to say. I can relate, given my own propensity for clumsy social interactions. I have said more than a few odd or off-key things in my lifetime.

It doesn't make me angry when people say stuff like "I am so sorry". It strikes me more like I think it might strike Dr. Spock, the character from Star Trek. "Hmmmm. Fascinating!"

I think to myself, "What are you talking about? I hit the jackpot." My life circumstances, over many years, have served to, slowly, very slowly, repair a lot of deeply flawed thinking on my part.

I originally thought that success in life meant becoming wealthy and important. Today, I experience tremendous gratitude when I say to friends and acquaintances, "I didn't become wealthy or important, I got rich instead." I know that sounds cliché, but I promise you that is my experience and that is my truth.

It also seems to me, that when someone says, "I am so sorry", that there can only be something apologize for if something wrong has actually occurred.

When my son, and my daughter were born, I assure you, something very right happened in my life, and something very good happened for humanity.

I won't beat a dead horse, here. I will just say that I hope that my book, and my foundation can help to radically flip this script.

It is my hope that, over time, "I am so sorry" can be permanently replaced with, "Fascinating! Tell me more!"

Opportunity

Chapter 19

The Numbers

I always say it is the humanity, first and foremost, that drives me in this mission. If the number of individuals on the Autism Spectrum were only one person, I would have the same level of passion. The prospect that this message of Simplicity is one that can be helpful to others is just icing on the cake.

The current rate of ASD diagnosis in the United States is estimated to be 1 in 59 according to the CDC as of 2018. As a rounded number, that equals .017 of the population. You can see this link for refrence:https://www.autism-society.org/what-is/facts-and-statistics/

Keep in mind, a ratio of 1 in 59 falls well within the bell curve of what is considered to be **normal.**

The USA population as of November 10, 2019 was listed as 329,968,629. Here is the reference link with that information:

https://en.wikipedia.org/wiki/Demography_of_the_United_States

With those numbers as a baseline, the USA population that is represented on the Autism Spectrum equals 5,576,469.

It is estimated that 65% of individuals on the Autism Spectrum are classified within the Level 1 and Level 2 categories. These are individuals who are capable and available for participation and contribution to the workforce.

Current estimates indicate that **90% of the individuals on the Autism Spectrum are unemployed or underemployed.**

65% of the Autism Syndrome Level 1 and Level 2 population within the USA equals **3,624,704 people.**

90% of Level 1 and Level 2 individuals on the Autism Spectrum equals roughly **3,262,233 individuals** in the USA who are unnecessarily unemployed or under-employed.

Without repeating all of those numbers again, using relative numbers, the potential local impact of that 90% group to the Dallas/Fort

Worth metro area alone equals *41,446 individuals who are unemployed or underemployed, and available.

These numbers are big. This is a lot of people. This is all around us. This is, in fact, Us.

*Link: https://en.wikipedia.org/wiki/Dallas-Fort_Worth_metroplex

Chapter 20

The Workplace

I occasionally attend support group meetings for adult individuals diagnosed on the Autism Spectrum.

At one recent meeting, I was speaking with a friend about her work situation. She is 27 years old, married, attractive and not a person that you might assume at first glance to be on the Autism Spectrum.

She is a research biologist by training, however after entering that field of work she realized that the work that she really loves is code writing.

She spoke to her husband about this. He fully supported her in leaving her research position to take an entry level position as a code writer.

She now works for an upstart tech company, one that utilizes an open office format to encourage collaboration. On most days, she finds that the open office environment is really distracting.

She told me that there are some days when she is able to block out all of the activity around her. On those days, she gets so locked into her work that when she looks up, it might be 6:30 or 7:00 PM in the evening. She often finds herself alone in the office, and she will have no idea when her associates went home.

In other words, she is totally locked in on those days, and she is super productive on those days.

She told me that her bosses have no idea how happy she would be if she could work in a basement, in a corner, alone, 95% of the time. She said that she isn't going to say anything to management about it though. Since she is entry level, she doesn't want to cause trouble. She wants to get some experience at this company, and then she will seek out a company that has a better working situation for her.

Think about that, she is smart, motivated, passionate and very talented. Her current company will likely lose her, and they will never really know why they lost her.

The solution is simple, and it is guaranteed to work. Ask your employees, all of your employees, especially your employees who are on the Autism Spectrum, "What can we do to help you be more comfortable and more successful in your job?"

Many companies are beginning to ask every employee these sorts of questions. Those companies that are proactively tailoring better work situations are seeing big benefits. As it relates to Autism specifically, many companies continue to lack confidence in asking these sorts of questions.

For businesses and workplace environments that will boldly pursue this information and will support highly practical, and legit, accommodations, the rewards really are off the charts.

Ask the questions. Embrace the answers. Implement the solutions. In doing so, you will unleash passion and talent beyond measure; Some of the greatest passion and some of the greatest talent that this world has known, in fact.

We truly are sitting on a gold mine here people!

Chapter 22

Thank You

Over the past two years, there were a number of times that I considered walking away from this project. "My hands are too full with daily responsibilities. It is time for me to act like a responsible grown up again and take sales job. I am just another traveler in this sea of humanity, what makes me think I should be the one doing this? I am done with this, glad that's over, now, time to get on with life!" Questioning and doubt show up in a lot of different ways.

Those same days that I would wash my hands of this project and put it behind me, I would usually go out and do some Uber driving in the evening. I would find myself consumed again, exuding passion and encouragement for an individual on the Spectrum, a parent, family member, friend, teacher, etc., etc.

I seems like I kept quitting and God kept not getting that memo. I am very grateful for that today.

It may seem like the message that I am promoting, for greater acceptance and inclusion, is a message that you can find in 100 other books on Amazon.

I believe the idea behind this book is a much larger statement to be honest. The stigma about Autism, and about cognitive differences in general, is less than it used to be, yet when you step back and take a clear-eyed look, stigma remains.

Today's stigma has softer packaging and better branding, if you will, but when we cut to the core, the assumption that Autism, and cognitive differences in general, represent a diminished opportunity to live full, meaningful and gratifying lives, is still alive and well.

I believe that the biggest reason for societal reluctance to take this major step forward in the Autism conversation is that society has needed permission from within the Autism community in order to do so.

I, myself, needed permission. And I have lived this Autism journey up close and personal. I was intimidated by the idea of promoting a hopeful and optimistic message about Autism.

I did thousands of focus groups before I could even start writing this book because I needed the sort of confidence that can only come from evidence. I still expect to get some blowback on this message of optimism, but today, after all of the legwork and research, I am eager to engage with my most adamant detractors.

These are the people that I thought about most before I began to write, and these are the people that I still think about the most today. Often, these are people who are on the front line, sharing a life journey with the Autistic individuals who are most significantly impacted by their sensory differences.

It is my hope that this group of people are those who will be most encouraged by this message of simplicity, and of universal understanding that is the basis of this book.

I challenge each of us to always remember that **every** Autistic individual that you will encounter, regardless of the level of Autism Sensory Impact, is a whole and complete person, on every level, and in every way, every time, no exceptions.

That Autistic person in front of you, **really is you.** My hope is that we will always be fascinated and intrigued, that we will embrace possibilities, and that we will celebrate humanity without restraint.

Thank you for reading my book. I hope that you have found, within these chapters, fresh insight that will elevate your bond with the amazing Autistic individuals who will enrich your life, throughout your life.

Please take a moment to post a rating for this book. Ratings are the most effective way for this book to be found by others who are seeking encouraging and hopeful information about Autism.

If you have further questions, or would like to connect please feel free to reach me via email at: Tony@autismsimplified.org

For more information speaking engagements, please visit my website.
www.autismsimplified.org